I0846338

The WORLD OF HORSES

By :NATHANIEL TRAGER

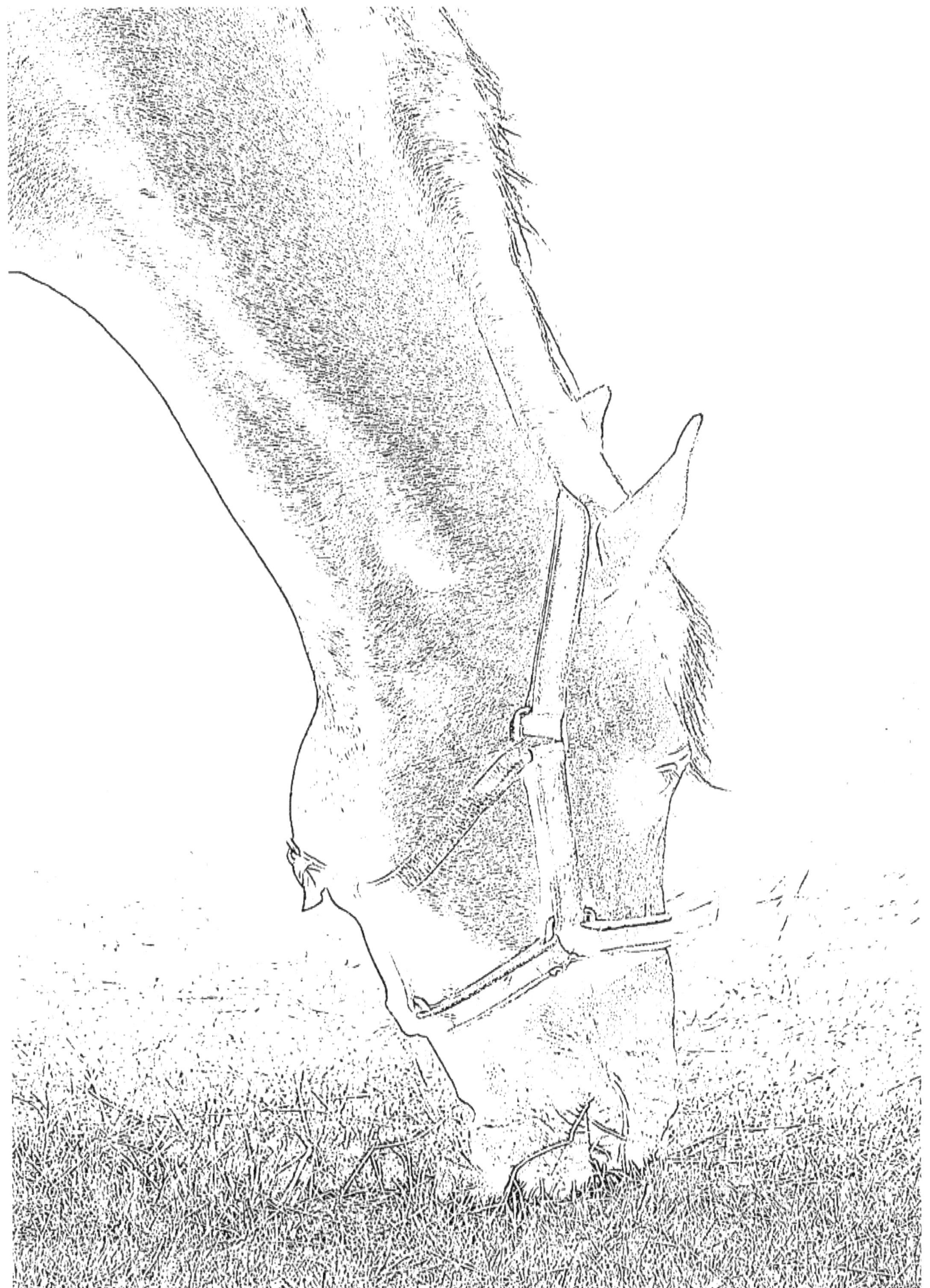

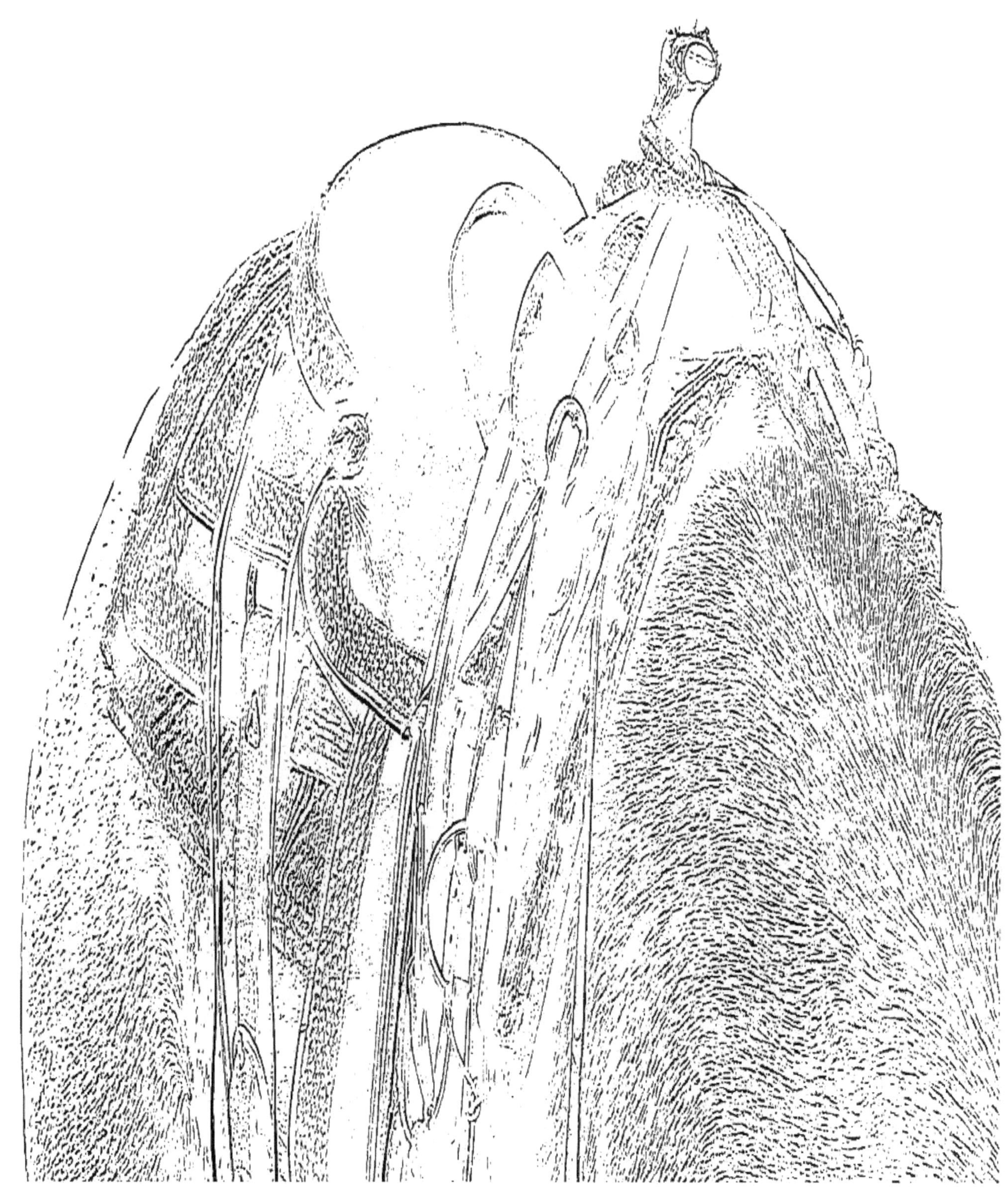

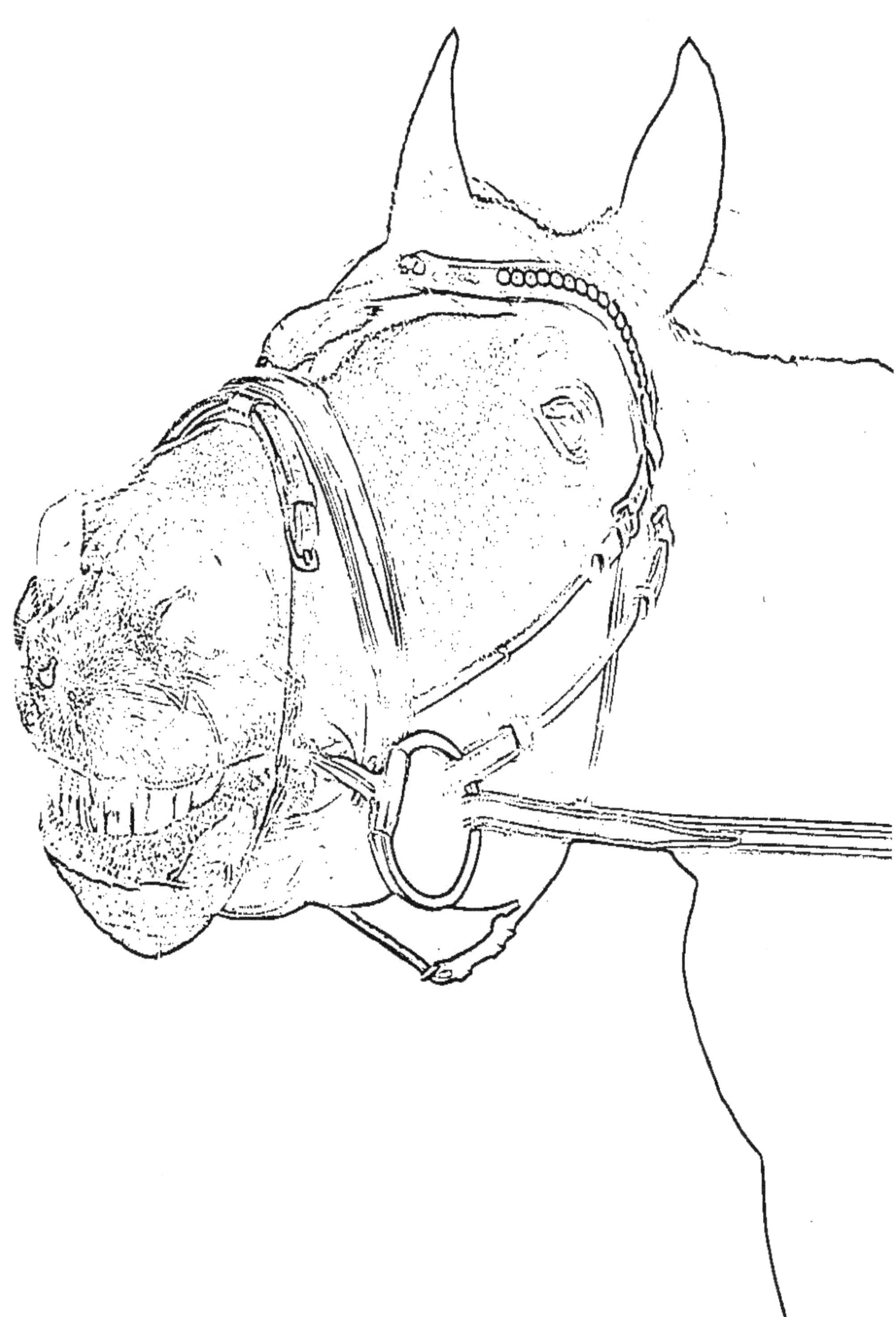

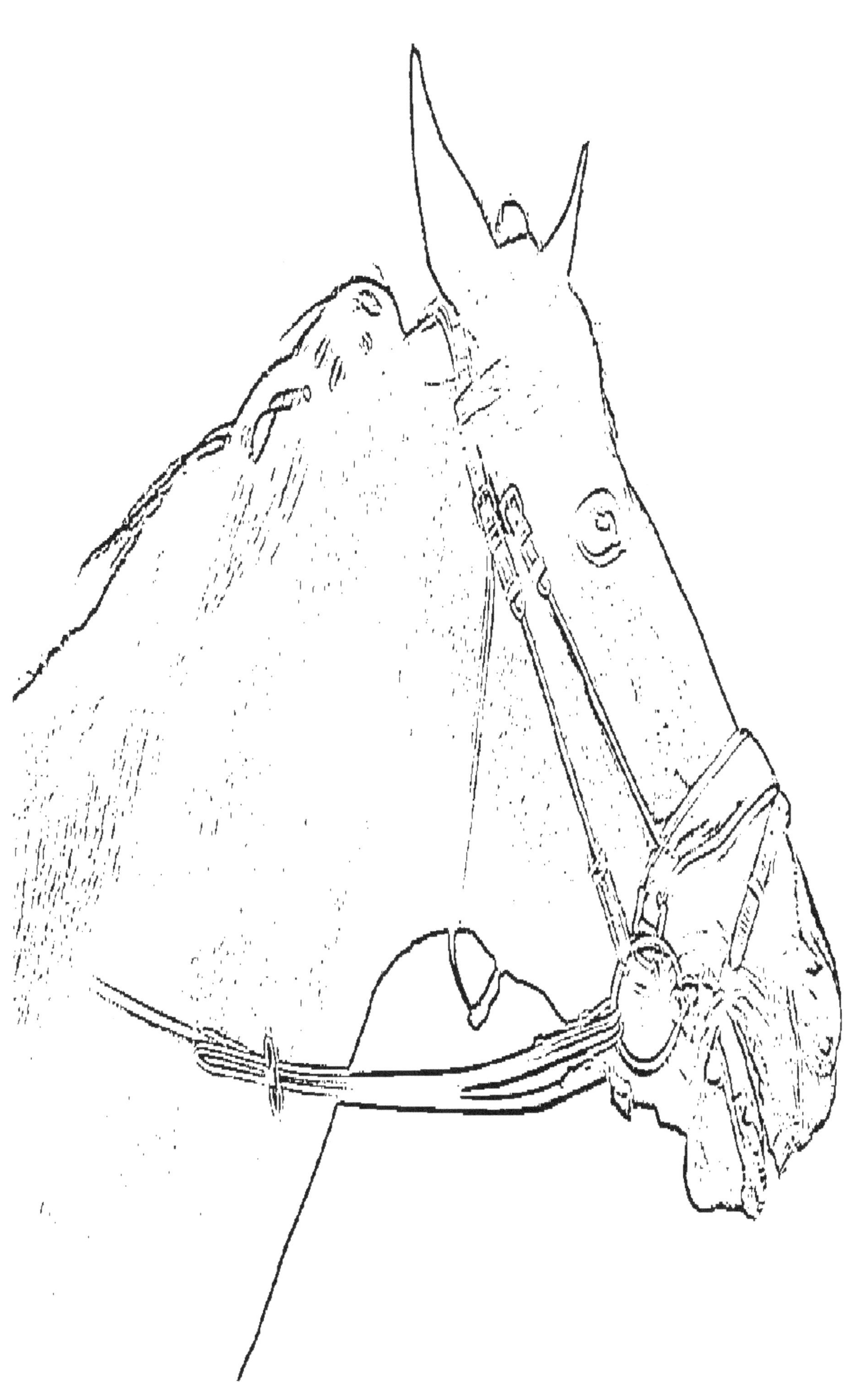

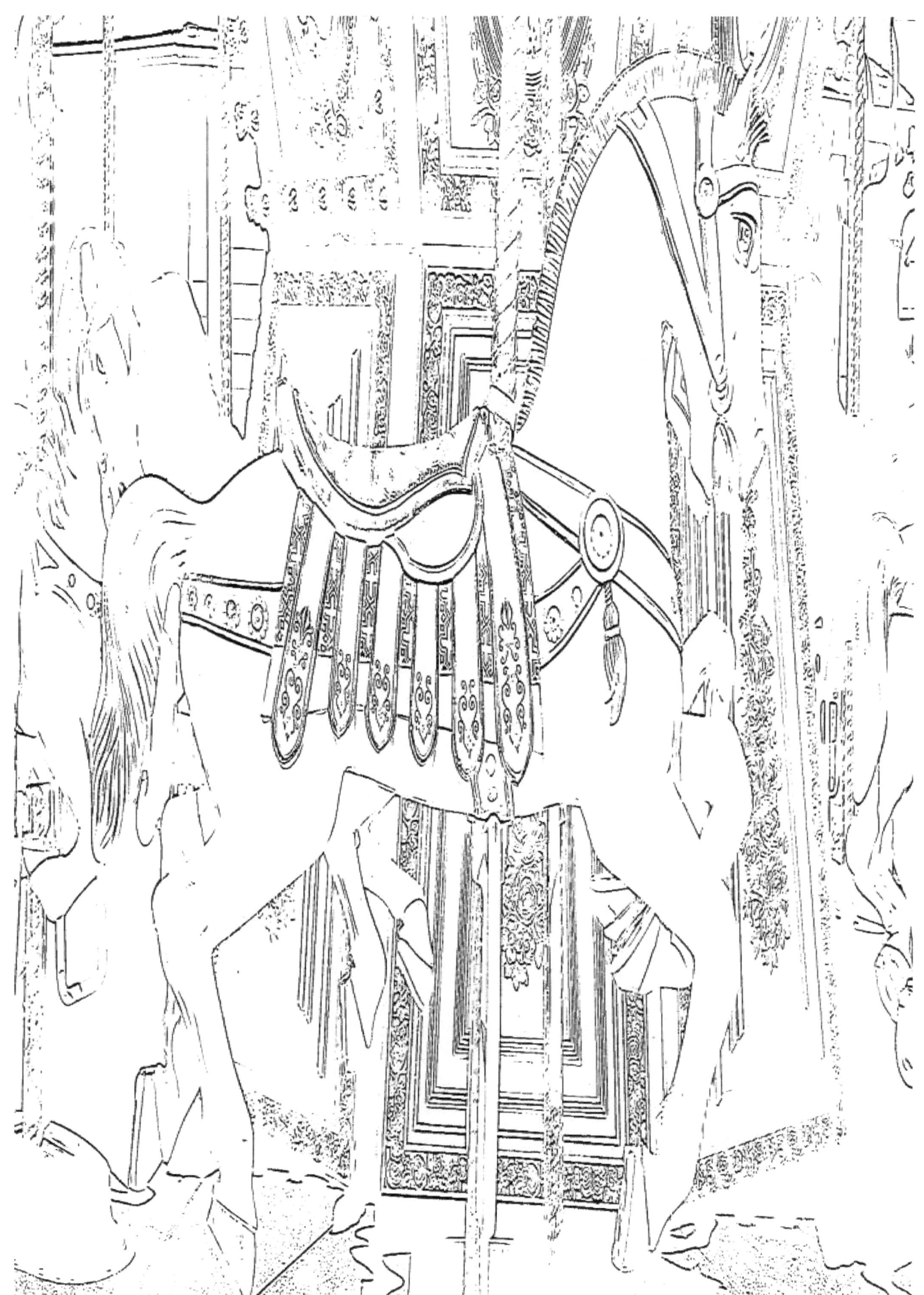

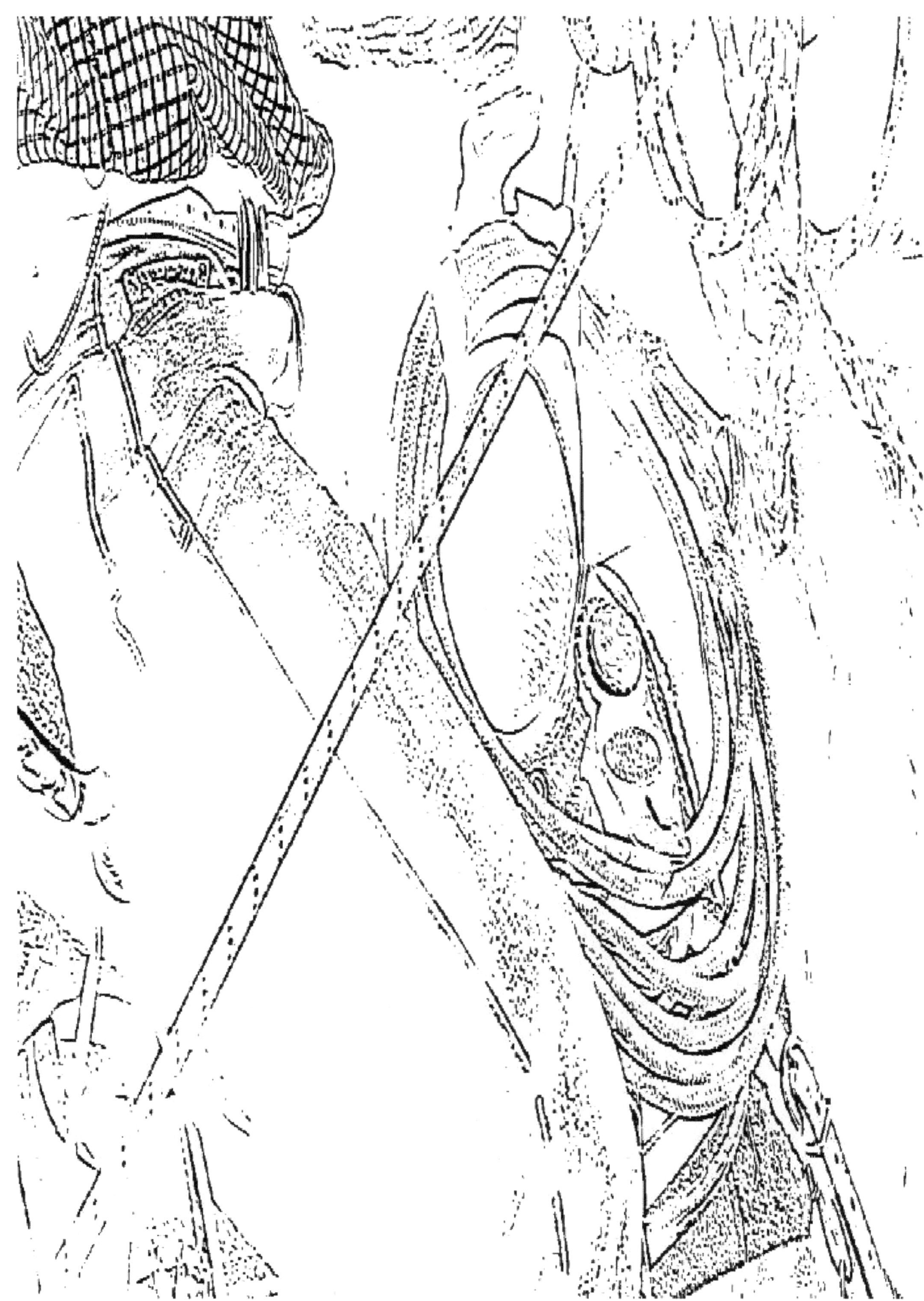

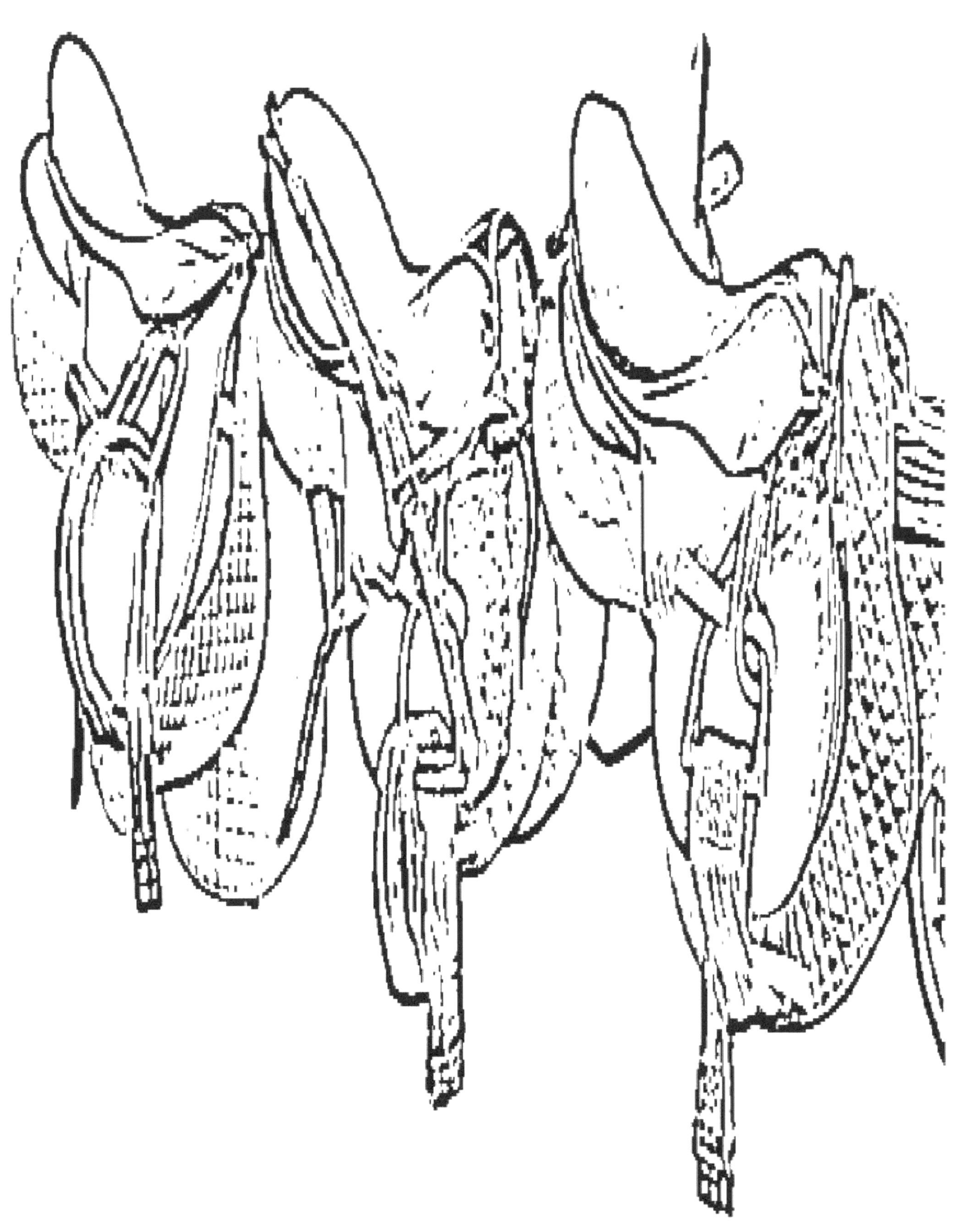

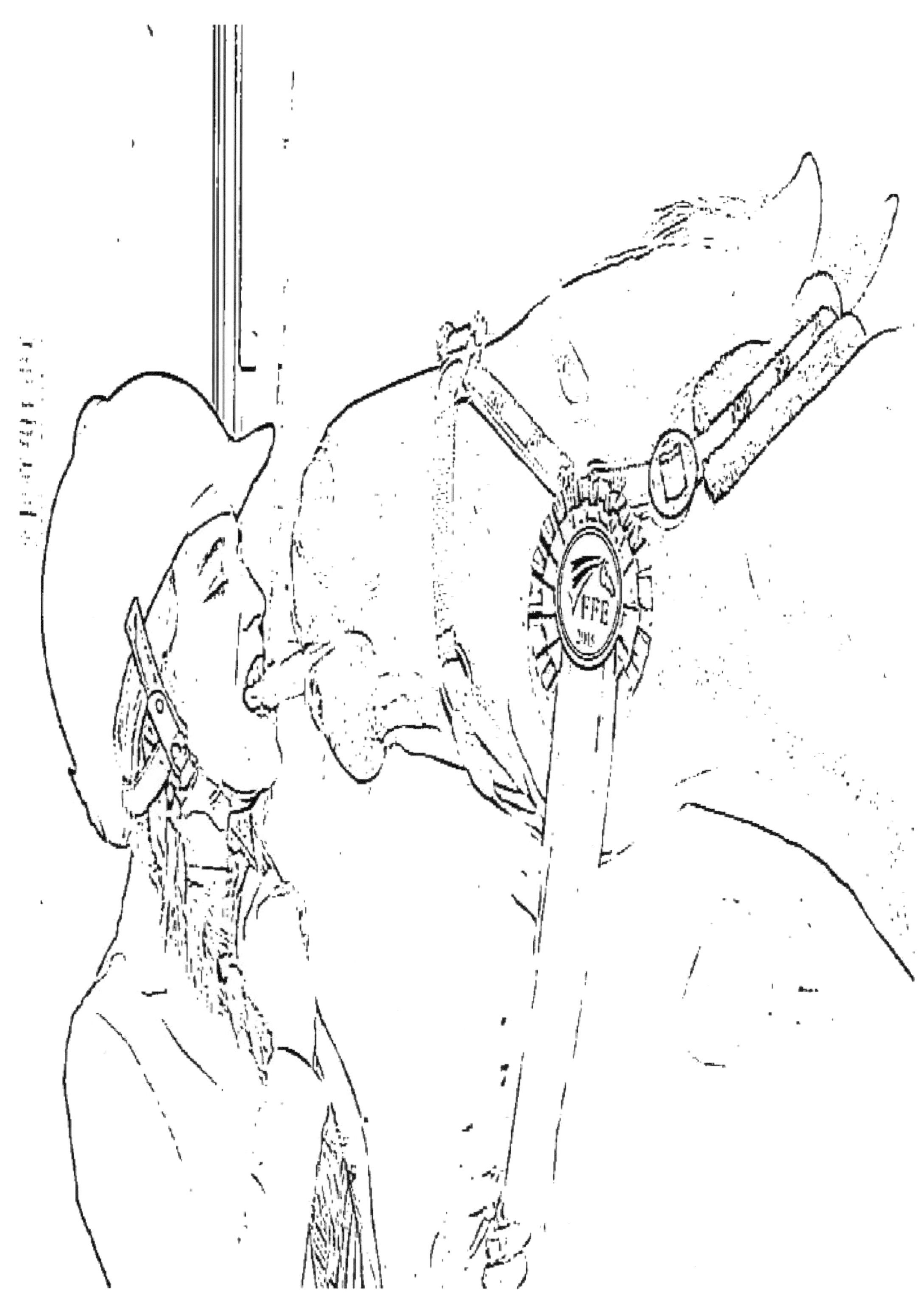
FFE

Berni

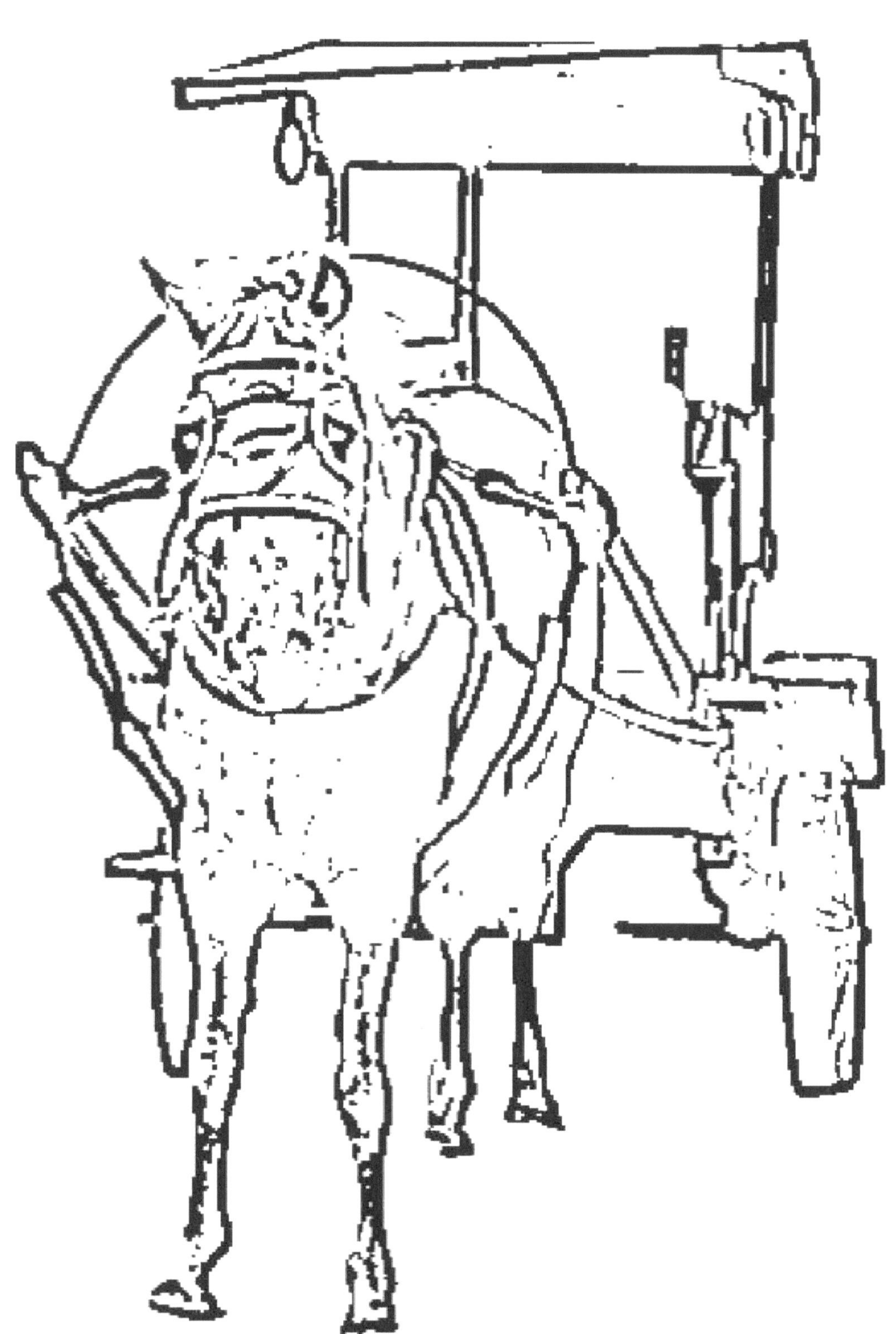

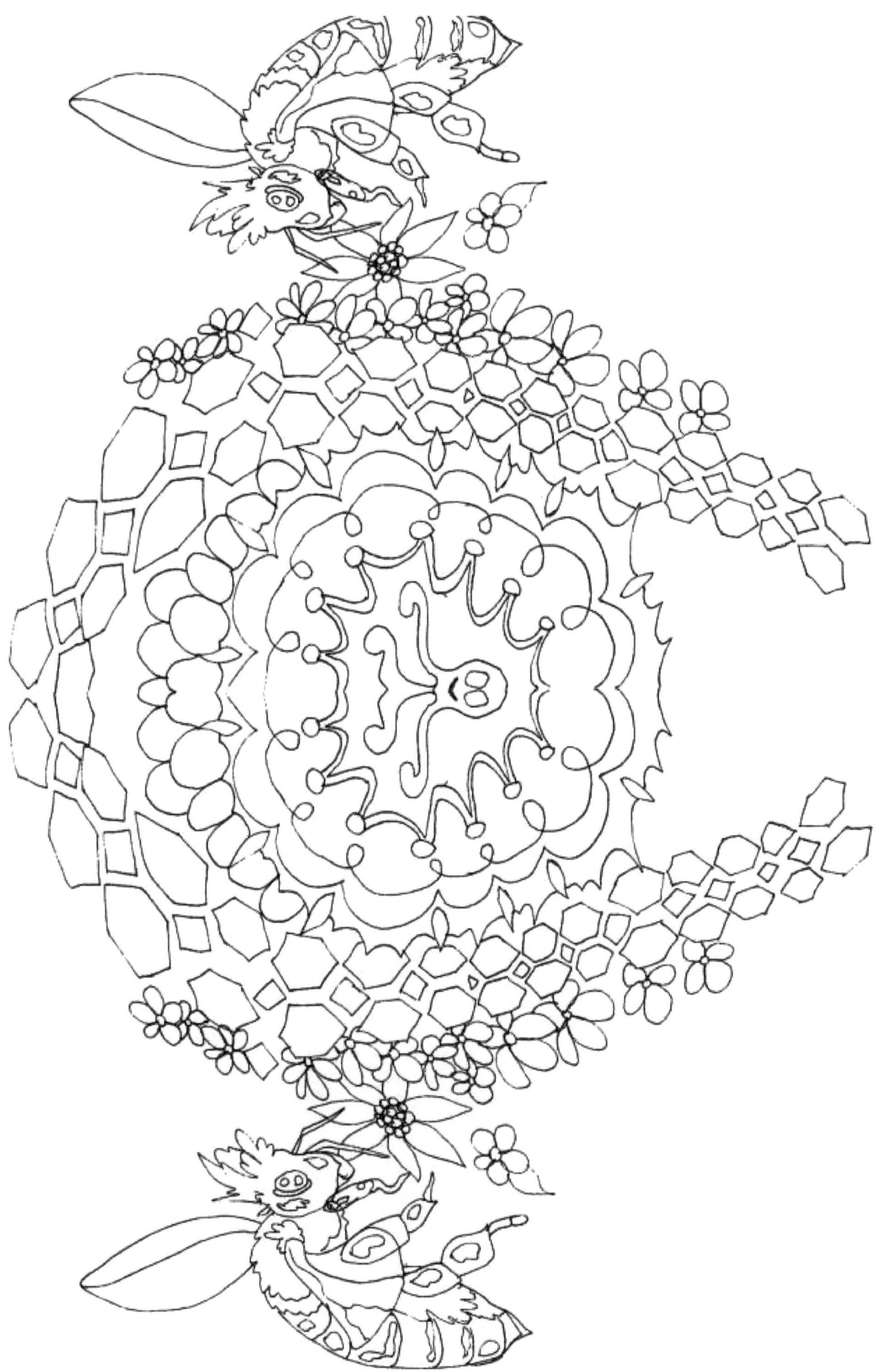

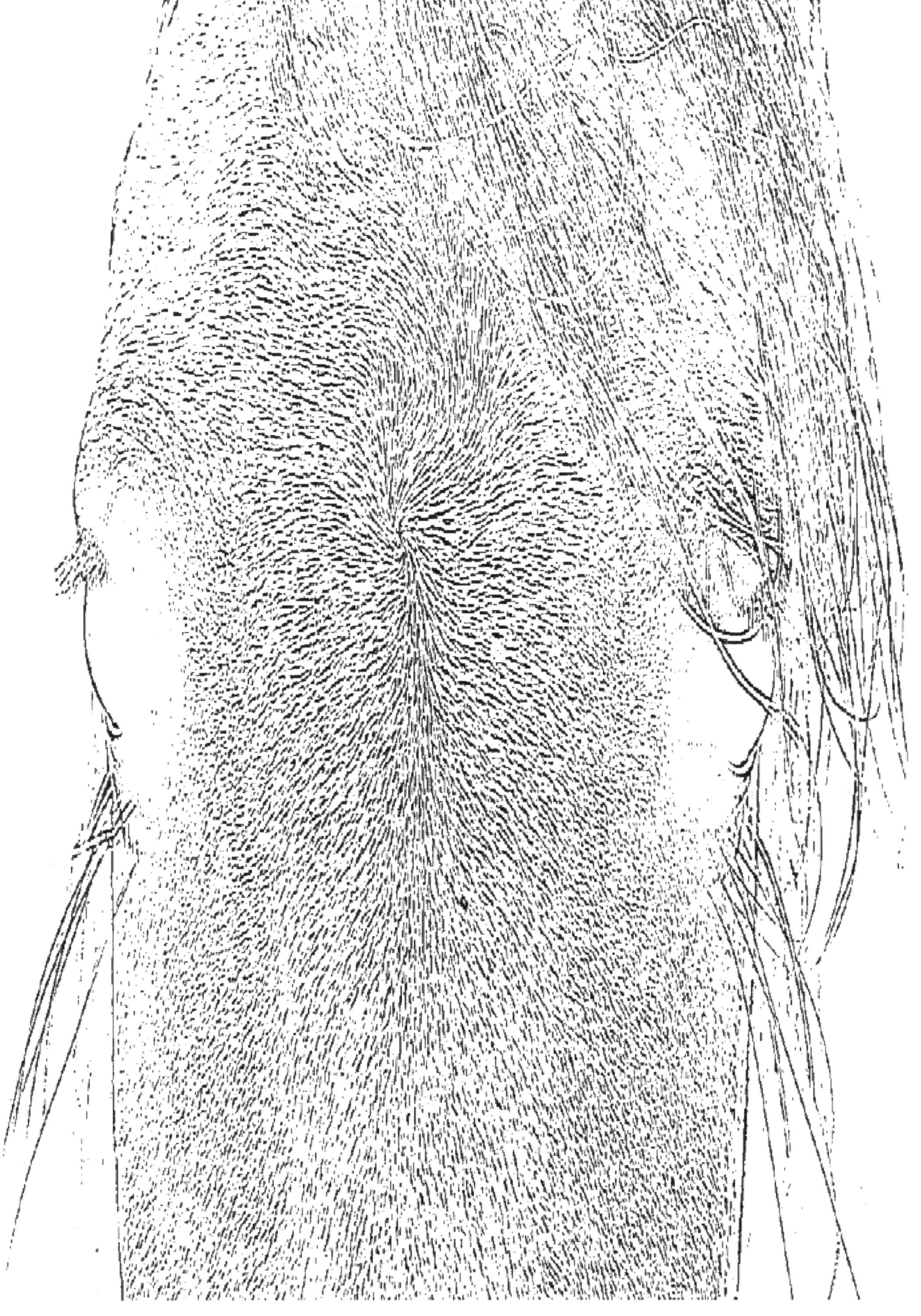

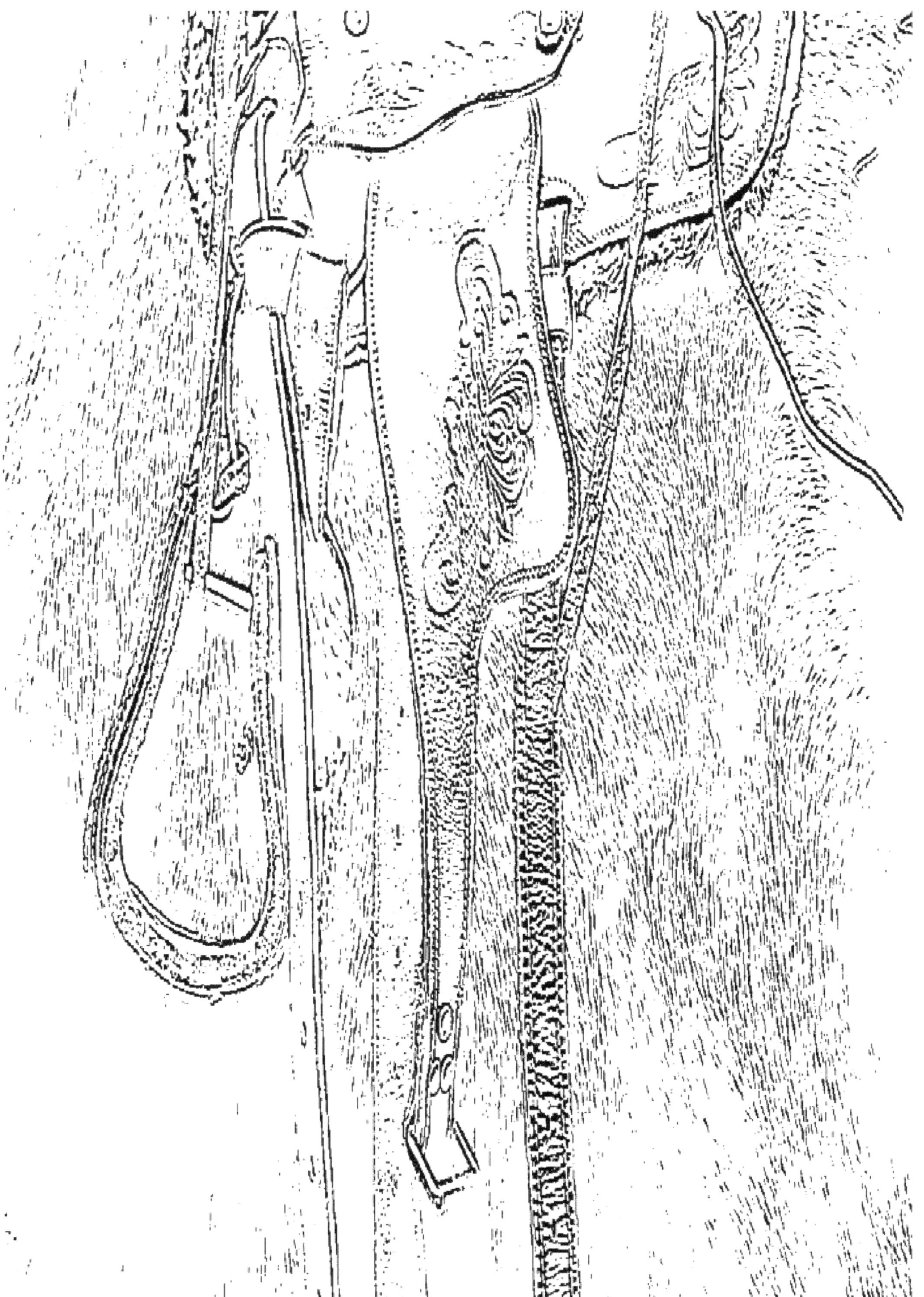

THE PRESERVE
AT THE RANCH
PRESCOTT
LAND & CATTLE
OKLAHOMA
17

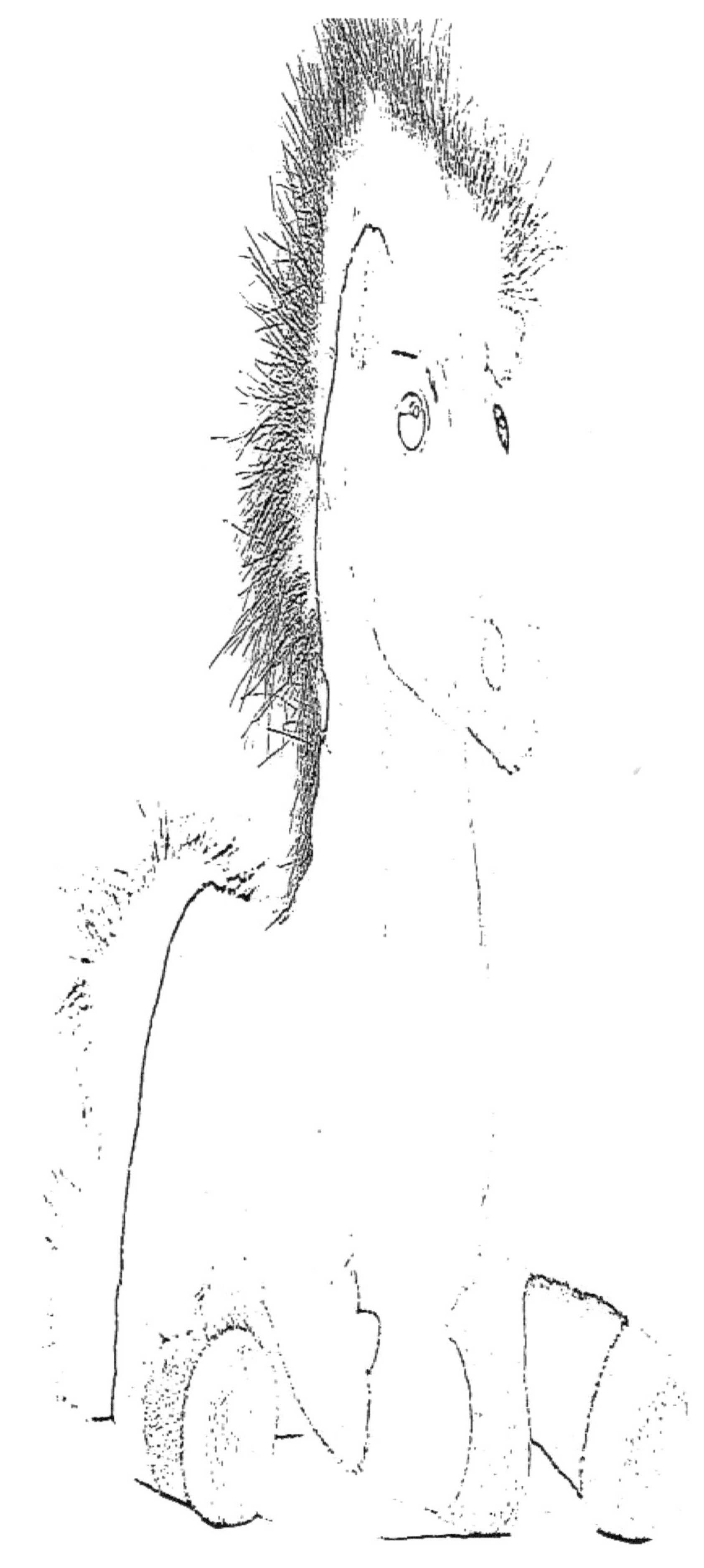

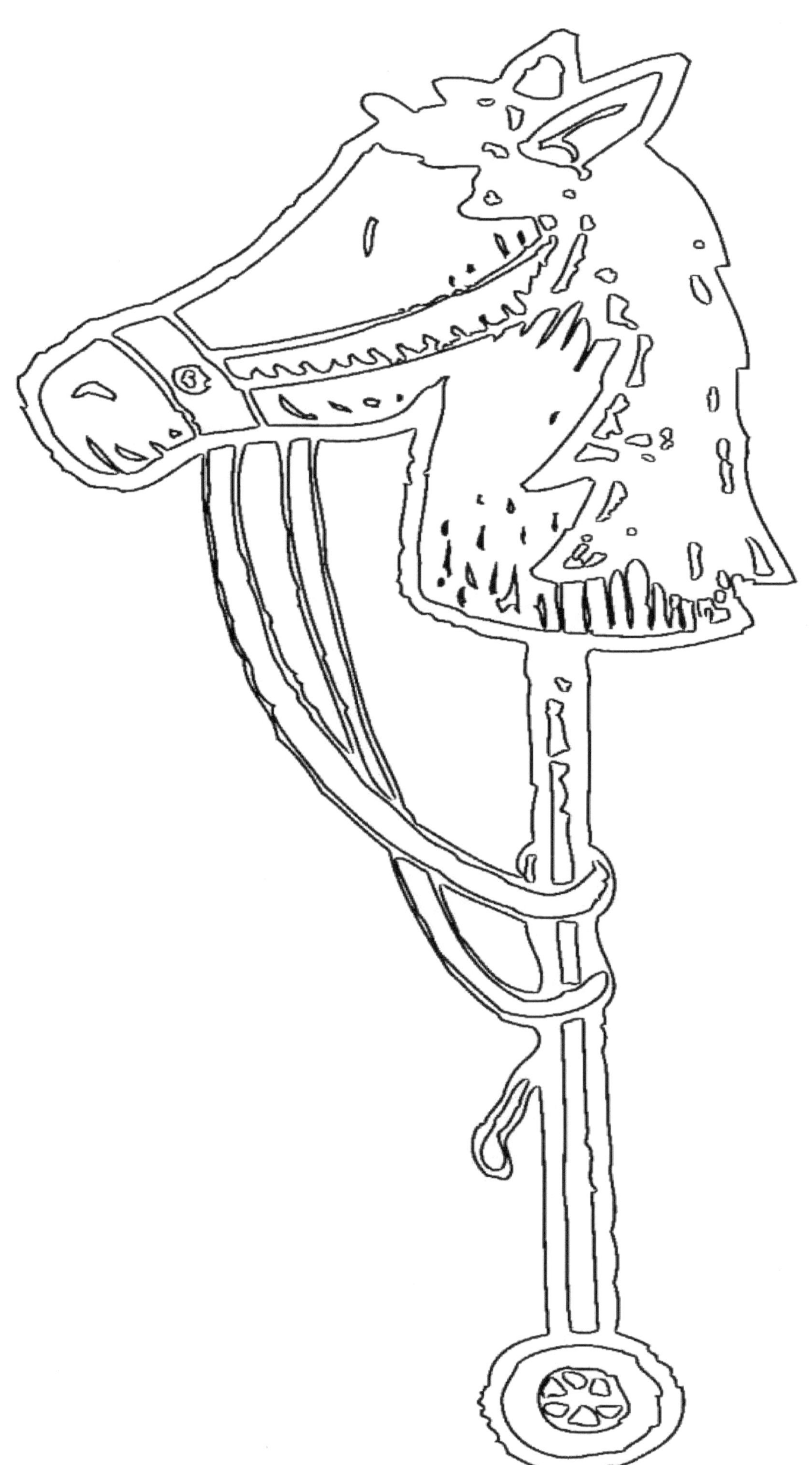

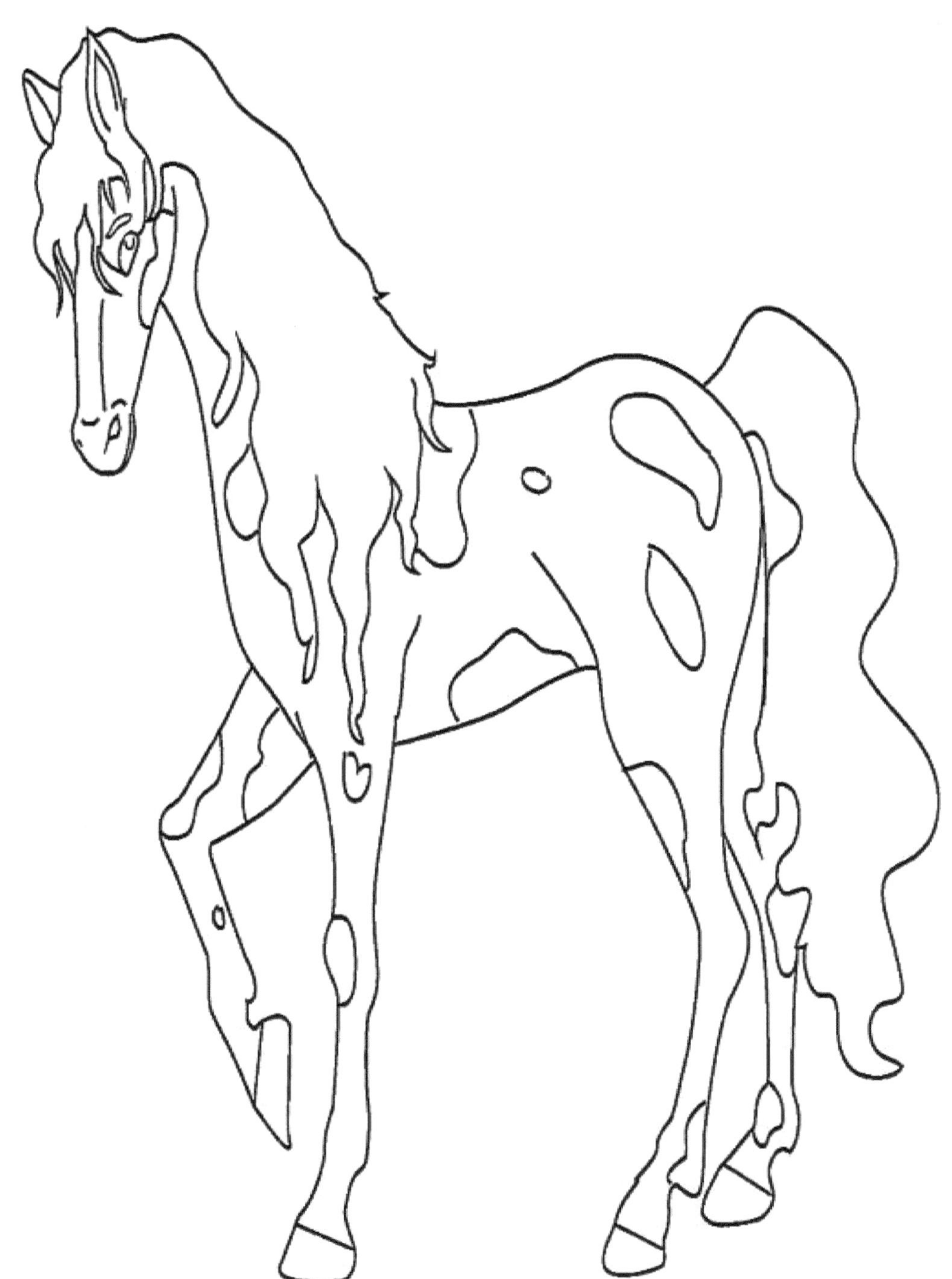

thank you for

your interested